Thiana

Avdela—A Macedonian Village in the Northwestern Greece
—Thiana's Native Land

Thiana

Avdela—A Macedonian Village in the Northwestern Greece
—Thiana's Native Land

BOOK I
2nd Edition

BY
REA-SILVIA COSTIN, P.E.

Thiana
AVDELA—A Macedonian Village in the Northwestern Greece
—Thiana's Native Land
Copyright © 2019 by REA-SILVIA COSTIN, P.E.

All rights reserved. No part of this publication may be reproduced, distributed, or transmitted in any form or by any means, including photocopying, recording, or other electronic or mechanical methods, without the prior written permission of the publisher or author, except in the case of brief quotations embodied in critical reviews and certain other noncommercial uses permitted by copyright law.

Although every precaution has been taken to verify the accuracy of the information contained herein, the author and publisher assume no responsibility for any errors or omissions. No liability is assumed for damages that may result from the use of information contained within.

Library of Congress Control Number: 2019908888
ISBN-13:   Paperback: 978-1-950073-61-0
            ePub: 978-1-950073-62-7

Printed in the United States of America

GoToPublish LLC
1-888-337-1724
www.gotopublish.com
info@gotopublish.com

CONTENTS

INTRODUCTION xi

Chapter 1	The ***Cambara*** (The Church Bell) 1
Chapter 2	Bechiul 7
Chapter 3	The Viper 11
Chapter 4	***Furii*** (The Thieves) 15
Chapter 5	Migdala 19
Chapter 6	Iani 21
Chapter 7	The Easter Picnic 25
Chapter 8	Thana, The Mail Bride 27
Chapter 9	Kiaua 31
Chapter 10	Turtukoaia 33
Chapter 11	Salonika 37
Chapter 12	Costin 41
Chapter 13	The Courtship 43
Chapter 14	Olga 47
Chapter 15	The Engagement Party 51
Chapter 16	Salonika II 55
Chapter 17	Tirgoviste 59
Chapter 18	The Hospital 61
Chapter 19	The Russian Soldier 65
Chapter 20	The Train 67

Chapter 21	Gorg...	71
Chapter 22	The Freight Train	75
Chapter 23	Gully al Spanou...	79
Chapter 24	The Iron Curtain	83
Chapter 25	Bucharest	85
Chapter 26	Cucotul al Sioutzouki	89

THIS BOOK IS DEDICATED TO THE MEMORY OF
MY MOTHER:

STELIANA SIOUTZOUKIS COSTIN

AND HER BELOVED NATAL LAND—AVDELA

To Mother:

"I've had these suits for twenty years,"
Mother said, pointing out to the neatly
hanging suits, looking as good as new.
"How can anyone wear same suits for twenty
years?" I was silently wondering,
a small girl looking up to my mother.

Now, the suits are still neatly hanging
in the closet.
My mother is gone… Me… a grown woman.
Now, I dream of Mother,
like I dream of her every night,
wearing a big, straw hat with a green ribbon,
a flowery, spring dress,
my mother young, her face smiling,
walking on a green pasture…
"She always liked hats,
she always liked walking," I was thinking,
"I'm so glad she's happy over there,
She doesn't have to wear the suits any longer."

Introduction

Have you ever given any thought as to why certain nations migrate, continuously changing where they live, while others are content to remain in the same place?

There are Nations known throughout the history as "the migratory or nomad nations," like the Gypsies, the Mongolians or, the Macedonians, just to name a few.

Why do these nations and people move to other places?

These nations and people are restless, and need to continuously change—they have the desire to improve, the desire to see new places, the courage and determination to seek a better life for them and for their families.

And then of course, there are the adventurous people that live for the trill of the unknown—even the danger that comes with it. They are the explorers and finders of new frontiers.

What about "destiny?" Have you ever given some thought about destiny? Is there even such a thing as "destiny?" Is our life predestined by a force bigger than we are? Is our life mapped out before we are even born? Did you ever try to change the course of your life, or the circumstances of it, to no avail? Did you go with the flow, so to speak, or did you tried to change it?

No straight answers to those questions exist that I know of. Each one of us is embarking on life's journey and trying to do the best one can. Each of us has our own story, our own yet-to-be-determined destiny.

Thiana is the first book of a trilogy that spans the lives of three generations of strong women: Calliope, the author's grandmother, who lived in Avdela, a village in northwestern Greece; Thiana, the author's mother, who made her life's journey from Avdela to Romania and married a Romanian man, Costin; and the author herself, who migrated from Romania via Greece, to the USA.

It is a saga of a family striving to find a better life.

The events, the stories, and the characters are real.

Here is Thiana's True Story.

Chapter 1

The *Cambara* (The Church Bell)

Thiana opened her eyes and glanced around. The great room was frigid. The sturdy, wooden window shutters were all wide open and the cold, brisk, mountain air invaded the room. Golden rays of sun streamed through the open shutters and tickled her face, not really warming the air. She could see her own breath forming like a small, white cloud coming out from her nose and mouth. She burrowed deeper into the wall bed, her small, thin body lost within the white *flocata*, the thick wool blanket that covered her up to her nose.

The great room had wooden beds, *canapeles,* built along all four walls. The room was paneled with hand-carved pine wood the color and smoothness of honey. Lions and intricate leaf design were carved on the doors of the armoire, also built into the wall. Thick red and blue woolen handwoven pillows, filled with dried, sweet-smelling ferns, covered the canapeles. Everybody in the house slept on the canapeles with flocates covering them up.

In the middle of the great room was the big wooden table with its short legs. There, the entire family had their meals, crouched on the floor and sharing the food from the big cooper trays.

On the far corner, next to the open window, a small wooden table and chair looked strange and out of place. It was her oldest brother Take's "place" to study. An oil lamp on Take's table was the only light source in the house besides the candle that flickered beneath the Aghia Maria's icon on the wall.

Thiana was alone in the great room. She heard the cambara, the church bell, ringing and wondered why.

Slowly, the recent events played back into her head. That year, 1920, she'd come to Avdela with the first arrivals along with her father and her cousins in April, a month before they usually came to Avdela, to clean and air the house in preparation for Easter. Her mother, her sister Maritza, and her brothers, Take, Toli and Vangheli, were to follow later that month.

She rose from the bed and found shiny new black shoes next to her bed and a new black dress in the armoire. She dressed, put the shoes on her woolen stockinged feet and went outside. She was a skinny little girl of not yet six with big soulful brown eyes and thick curly brown hair cut straight at the earlobes. "If the cambara rang, something of importance must've happened," Thiana thought. She had to join the family and the crowd gathered in the church's front yard, *perivoli*.

Their house was the last one at the top of the hill. A narrow path separated their front yard from the Aghiou Athanase's Church. She left the house. At the back, the cool breeze moved through the old pecan tree's leaves. Birds sang. She crossed the road from their yard to the church. The Aghiou Athanase Church, white with thick plastered brick walls, was the last building up the hill. The church itself was not very large. The inside was dark and cool with candelas flickering beneath the heavy ornate icons.

Every time the church cambara rang, the village people gathered in the perivoli.

* * *

Avdela was a small community that consisted of about two hundred *Armani,* or Macedonians. The Greeks were not welcomed into the community, even though the village was located in the Pindos Mountains of northwestern Greece.

There were several villages like Avdela, Perivolion, Smixi, Prosvoro, Samarina, Alatopetra in the mountains, with an exclusive population of Armani.

More than 2,200 years ago, Alexander the Great, the great king of Macedonia, overthrew the Persian Empire and carried Macedonian arms to India, and laid the foundations for the Hellenistic world kingdom.

Now, after the expulsion of the Turks in 1912, Serbia, Greece and Bulgaria divided Macedonia into three parts in 1913. There were also Macedonians established in Albania and Romania. The Macedonians in the northwestern part of Greece had their own language and culture, separate from the Greeks, even though they lived in the same countries.

Avdela was located about forty kilometers away from the nearest town, Grevena, and the only way to get there was by traveling on the *mules'* backs and horses', *cavala,* on the narrow mountain trails. It was a place for summers. From early April, before Easter, to late August after Aghia Maria's holiday, on August 15, the village people spent the summers in Avdela. The majorities of them were shepherds and owned flocks of ships and goats.

The village had five Orthodox Churches: Aghiou Athanase, Aghiou Triad, Aghiou Sotiriou, Aghiou Nicolas and Aghia Maria. It's said that Macedonia was the first place that Saint Paul stepped on European land when he came to preach the Holy Bible and spread the Christian religion.

The people of the village usually married within the village, or among other villages of Armani.

It was a close community, with customs as old as time and most were unwilling to change, unwilling to open to outside influences. The community had its own code of honor and justice. The Greek police never interfered with the conflicts of the community.

Each family took care for any crimes, thefts, or revenge. They all knew each other, their houses and their stories.

* * *

Thiana went to the Church to see what was happening. People dressed in finery filled the courtyard. Some wore traditional Greek costumes. The women wore full length pleated handwoven wool skirts, white shirts, and blue vests. The shirts and vests were hand embroidered with bright blue and red thread. Men had on an *aba*, an undershirt, made of handwoven folkweave woolen material, a smock of thick handwoven linen embroidered in the front, sleeves and skirt, and breeches of white broadcloth. The *kemer*, a girdle of twilled flame–colored wool with stripes, was worn with a black broadcloth waistcoat ornate with flame-colored trimmings, knitted socks, gathers, and slippers with cowhide straps, an astrakhan and velvet cap and a knife called "zhrenche." The older women and the widows wore black dresses and had their hair tightly bounded with black *mandiles,* or scarves.

People stared at Thiana as she passed. "Maybe they are admiring my new shoes," she thought. She'd never worn a pair of shoes before. "Father probably bought me the new shoes as a present for Easter. Maybe he brought them when he last went to Grevena with his load of lumber to sell them at the market."

Women made the sign of the cross, spitting onto their bosom, as if the devil himself were passing.

"Something is wrong," Thiana thought. "I have to find Take or Maritza or maybe Toli, to tell me what it is happening."

Finally, she found Take. Take was her oldest brother, the one who was going to school. He was twelve. He proudly wore the brown wool suit his mother had made for him, his thick brown hair greased and neatly combed over his forehead.

"Take, what's going on? Why is the cambara ringing? Why are those people making the sign of cross when I go by? Is it my new shoes they are so curious about?"

"No, no. You were very sick, for over a month. You had meningitis. Mother put you in the great room and opened all the shutters for the mountain air to clean your head. We all thought you were going to die. Everybody gave up hope."

"That's why father bought me new shoes? To bury me, in? And the new dress too?" Thiana felt shocked.

"Yes, and the new dress too."

"That's why the cambara was ringing? They thought I died?"

"That's true. Everybody had given up hope for you."

"I'm well now and I'm glad about the shoes and the new dress. Easter is coming and I'll wear them to church and to the dance."

She felt good, healthy and full of life. The sun shined brightly and the air smelled of pine.

Chapter 2

Bechiul

Thiana's mother, Calliope, a tall, beautiful, willowy, woman had hazel eyes and long chestnut hair that she wound into two thick, tight braids that she pinned on top of her head like a crown. When she was sixteen years old, Iani, Thiana's father, stole her from her parents' house on his horse's back. Later, he married her. The two families were neighbors, their houses next to one another in Avdela.

There were five children in the family, Thiana and her older sister Maritza and three brothers: Take, Toli and the youngest, Vangheli.

The family's main residence was in Grevena, a predominantly Turkish town. When the Turks had to leave the town for the population exchange, around 1912, her father bought a great stone house form a Turkish family that was leaving the village. The house had thick walls and tall stone walls that surrounded the yard with great, locked, wooden gates. The house had a stone *jakie*, or fireplace, upstairs and balconies from the rooms upstairs overlooked the back yard. There, they had fruit trees and a small vegetable garden that her mother tended to.

Thiana remembered the Turkish family that lived across the street from them in Grevena. The Turkish women wore a veil covering their faces at all times and looked at the outside world through windows covered with intricate wood designs, such that nobody from outside could see them. She remembered hearing that the Turkish women dyed their hair with dye made from boiling the green shells of pecans and they colored their toes and fingernails with red carmine. They remained inside their houses waiting for their husbands to return from the fields and waited for them at the door to wash their feet before entering the houses.

In the beginning, her father owned flocks of sheep and Thiana remembered seeing him making cheese: he put the sheeps' milk or the goats' milk into big round barrels, added the ferment, and the next day he cut big pieces of white cheese and stored them. Her father, as Thiana remembered him, was a short, stocky man with big, rough hands.

Later, her father sold the sheep and bought five horses to use for his lumber trade. The horses had names and the children fondly took care of them, walking them to pasture, cleaning them, and riding them on their bare backs. They were good, strong, unpretentious horses trained to carry heavy loads on the narrow mountain trails.

One cold, winter evening, in the great room downstairs in their house in Grevena, while Thiana helped her mother comb the dyed wool and spin it in a narrow, uniform thread preparing it to be woven into a rug, Calliope started to spin her stories.

"You know, when you were a little child, just a little baby, maybe six months old, I had you all bundled up in rugs and I tied you tightly on Bechiul's saddle. We were going to Avdela on horseback. A lot of other people traveled with us on the mountain path, including your father and your older brothers and sister and your father's cousins. Total of forty people, all riding on the horses' backs. The horses were loaded down with sacks hanging from both sides of the saddles. Your brothers and sister were tied up in front of you, each on a horse's back. It was still dawn. The night was cold and the sunlight had just started to creep above the horizon, gray at first. The fog was quite thick and one could not see the narrow path beyond a few meters.

"That sounds just like our trips now. There are times when you couldn't see more than a few meters in front of the horse."

"That's right. Nothing has changed, has it? Well, as the story goes, Bechiul suddenly stopped on the narrow path and wouldn't move. Your father went next to him trying to nudge him to go on. Talking to him as if he understood."

"But, he does understand. I know that for a fact. There are plenty of times when I talk to him. He understands what I'm saying to him."

"Yes, I know. It seems that way. Well, Bechiul would not move from the path and the rest of the caravan behind started to grow impatient and people told your father to whip him."

"To whip him? That's not possible. Bechiul is the kindest of all horses. He's getting old, that's all."

"You know your father better than I do. He won't whip his horses! Well, your father came closer to Bechiul, and looked carefully around him. Then, he noticed you on the ground beside the edge of the ravine."

"Oh! I'm glad he looked."

"Me too! Your binder loosened and you fell from the saddle. Bechiul knew and that was his way of letting us know. He saved your life."

"Yea! I knew it. That's why of all the horses, I love Bechiul best."

"Let's finish here and start to set up the table. Others will soon come and they'll be very hungry."

Another time Bechiul, the oldest of the five horses and almost blind, fell into the family's *private*, outhouse, at their home in Avdela, as he was grazing in the taller greener grass, and the entire family worked hard to get him out, pulling him out with ropes. The five horses were part of the family too.

Take was the only one going to school at the time, while also learning to help his father with his trade job. One time when his father took Take with him to the market, he proudly asked Take to figure out how much money he was supposed to get from the customer. By the time Take was finished counting, adding and subtracting and multiplying on paper, his father had all figured it out in his head, much more quickly and more accurately.

The family no longer owned a cow or sheep or goats, but Take had to have milk for breakfast. He was the only one of all children to drink milk before he went to school. Thiana ran all the way from their house on the top of the hill, down to the valley to a woman who owned a cow and bought a liter of milk. She carried the milk in a small pot, *caldarusa*, and brought it to Take. She would sit on a corner of the big room, quietly waiting for Take to finish his breakfast and maybe, maybe leave her a spoonful of milk.

Her father traveled with the horses, loaded with lumber, to town to sell lumber and boards from Avdela to Grevena or other neighboring villages. He'd bring back sacks of grains that he sold in the village.

They were not among the richest families of the community, the ones who owned sheep and land, but were not the poorest either.

They were a happy, close, family. Their love for each other was their greatest richness.

In Avdela, they also had a vegetable garden in the back yard that her mother and Maritza tended. They cultivated pole beans, onions, potatoes, and greens. Manulus Zarma was her first cousin on her father's side. His house was the next one down the mountain from theirs. He went up to the spring called the "Shopot al Damashoty" and hand dug a ditch, bringing water from the spring down first to their garden, then to his garden farther down the mountain. After the two gardens were water fed, he went up the mountain again and dammed the newly dug ditch until the next time the gardens needed to be watered.

In Avdela, Thiana and her sister Maritza would go into the nearby woods to gather sacks of pinecones for the fire. They had a big oven, *chireap*, built of stones in the backyard, where her mother baked bread once a week and sometimes made *pita*, pie. Pita was their treat.

Her mother cooked big trays—*tipsie* of pita filled with *urzici* or *vearza*—greens gathered from the backyard vegetable garden, and set it on the middle of the small table. They all sat on the floor around the table and ate their slice of pita, directly from the tray.

They couldn't be happier.

chapter 3

The Viper

Thiana and her sister, Maritza, gathered pinecones in the woods. Their mother sent them early in the morning with two big sacks. She needed pinecones and wood to heat up the chireap. Today was Friday, the day to bake bread.

Maritza was nine. She had thick, curly, ash-blond hair and a round face that seemed to be smiling all the time. The girls were barefoot.

Thiana walked the narrow path between the tall trees, pine needles tickling her bare feet, searching for cones, when a viper struck from the bushes. Thiana saw it first.

Small and thin as a finger, it was gray with a flat head marked with a black V. For a moment, Thiana stood transfixed. It seemed the viper stared at her too. Thiana opened her mouth to call her sister, but no sound came out. Like a bolt of lightning, the viper bit her bare foot.

Thiana fell unconscious.

Maritza heard her sister tumble to the ground and ran to see what had happened. Thiana's eyes were closed, her left foot red and beginning to swell. Maritza dropped her full sack of pinecones and ran as fast as she could, skirts in hands, back to the village.

"Help, somebody help my sister. A viper bit her foot," she started screaming, as soon as she reached the outskirts of the village.

"Hey, Maritza what happened?" A man ran out of his house.

"My sister, Thiana, she is in the woods, unconscious. I think a viper bit her foot."

"How do you know this?"

"Her foot started to swelled up and it's all red, by the time I left. Quick, help her!"

"I'll come with you. Stella," he called to his wife. "Let everyone know, what happened. Try to find Iani and bring him to the woods."

"Father is not home, yet. He is supposed to be back today, but he hasn't arrived."

The man ran back in the woods with Maritza. When they found Thiana, she was still lying on the ground, unconscious, her left foot badly swollen.

"Quick, come here." The man called Maritza. "Help me hold her leg up. I can see the two holes the viper's teeth left in her heel. I'll try to suck out the venom."

The man put her little sister's heel at his mouth and sucked the blood mixed with the viper's venom and spit it on the ground next to him.

"Come over here and try to hold her leg still on my thigh. Make sure she doesn't move," the man shouted to Maritza.

Maritza took her sister's leg in her arms and held it as tightly as she could on the man's thighs. He took a knife out of his back pocket and opened the blade. He wiped it across his thigh and then began to cut away at Thiana's heel.

Blood poured onto the pine needles and leaves covering the ground.

The village men came and stood around in a circle.

"Quick, somebody give me a chain, to tie her leg with," the man was asking.

"Here, I knew you'd need this," another man gave him a thick iron chain.

The man tied Thiana's ankle with the chain so that the infected blood wouldn't make it to her heart. The foot swelled more and more.

Everything they knew to do, they'd done. Now, it was up to God to save her.

Thiana was still unconscious. Even the sharp pain of the knife, cutting into her flesh, had not woken her.

The man took her in his arms and brought Thiana home with them.

By that time Thiana's father, Iani came home and found out about his daughter. He went outside and killed a young lamb. He put Thiana's foot inside the belly of the freshly slaughtered lamb. The foot was still swollen very badly and they were talking about amputation.

The second day when Thiana woke up, they took her foot out of the lamb. Her leg seemed miraculously healed, all white and back to normal size.

She was saved.

Chapter 4

Furii (The Thieves)

The winter months, the family spent in Grevena.

In the spring, the villagers went to Avdela and opened their summerhouses. The trip from Grevena to Avdela took three days. They loaded mules down with household goods. Food, water, and children road atop the mules or horses.

Thieves, *furi*, would await the caravans on the narrow paths to rob them of all their money.

One time, Thiana and her family were traveling from Grevena to Avdela and her father was carrying money from the lumber he'd sold in Grevena. He carried the money close to his body, in a *kemer*, a wallet inside his wide belt. The clothing for the men was the traditional Greek costume, the pleated white *fustanelles*—skirts on top of large white breaches tied with a wide, leather belt. They wore a loose white shirt tucked into the wide belt with a vest on top.

As they traveled the narrow path, Thiana's father made a sign with this hand for everyone to stop and be still.

"I smell cigar smoke ahead," her father whispered. "Probably there are *furi* waiting for us up ahead."

He took his money out of the Kemer and threw it inside the *ciumica*—a pot—with water that they carried on the saddle's side.

Thiana rode with her mother on the back of a horse. She saw the two masked men approaching on horseback. They stopped and slid down from their horses with guns pointed at them.

"Give me all your money, and you and your family will walk away unharmed."

"I have no money," Thiana's father's voice shook.

"You're lying. We know you sold your lumber at the market in Grevena and now you're going back to Avdela with the money from the trade. Give it to us."

"I have no money. Search all my sacks and if you find something, take it!" Thiana's father challenged.

The two men first searched Iani's wide belt and his inside pocket. They found nothing.

They looked everywhere, even inside the ciumica, but could not find anything. The money was stacked on the lateral wall of the ciumica that had a large bottom and narrow top.

Calliope, Thiana's mother, pinched Thiana so she would cry out loud. The harder her mother pinched, the louder she wailed. Calliope hoped that the furi would be afraid that the noises would draw attention to them.

"We'll leave you now, but we'll meet again." The two men departed.

"That was a close call," Calliope said with her shaking hand covering her mouth. "We were lucky that they wore masks and we couldn't see their faces. Otherwise, if we were to recognize them, they would have killed us."

"Father, you were so brave," Thiana said running toward her father with her arms wide open. "I almost peed in my panties. I was so scared."

But not everybody was so lucky, or had the same quick mind, as Thiana's father.

One story was that a husband and wife of the richest families in Avdela, the Niculescu, were attacked by furi on their way to Avdela. The furi knew they had money and decided to take the man hostage and ask for a ransom for his life. The wife, who was a teacher, asked the furi that they take her instead of her husband because her husband had a weak heart. She was afraid for him. The furi took her, bound her tight, and covered her head. They transported her on horseback to their hiding place in the mountains.

They sent word that they expected 200,000 drachmas for her safe return. At that time 200,000 drachmas could buy the entire village of Avdela. The woman was gone for over a month until her husband, who worked at a bank in town, could gather the required money. He left it in a locked case at the place where they'd instructed him to leave it. The furi returned the woman, unharmed. No one involved the Greek police in their problems.

People say that usually, the furi might be somebody who knows you very well, not a stranger at all. Furi were probably men from the village who knew when certain families are supposed to pass by with money on them. The furi covered their faces with black masks. Nobody knew who they were, but the furi often knew their victims and their habits.

This was certainly the case, when masked furi came during the night to Thiana's house, in Avdela.

Thiana's father had just bought freshly-ground wheat in sacks from the mill and had stacked them in the back room, next to the kitchen.

After everybody in the household went to sleep, the furi entered through the back window and stole a few sacks of the wheat. Calliope woke and saw the masked furi leaving with their stolen goods, but she kept silent. She knew if she said a word, or screamed, she would end up being killed.

The next morning, a trail of wheat led from their back window to their cousin's house.

Calliope never mentioned anything to her husband or anybody else. She didn't want her husband killed, over a sack of wheat.

She was too smart.

Chapter 5

Migdala

Thiana liked to visit different places. She didn't like to work in the garden with her mother and her sister, Maritza, or sew, or even cook. She wanted to see the world, or as much of it as she could. There was a restlessness within her that made her not able to stay put in one place for too long. She had a curiosity about the world in general and people in particular that she had to satisfy. She had an excess of energy.

She remembered insisting that she go with her father to visit his brother's family in Baiasa. Her father loaded his horses to go to Baiasa's open market and took her with him. They had to go across the large river on a makeshift ferryboat. The boat was made of logs tied together to form a huge platform, and the man in charge of it pulled a rope around two pulleys to drive the ferryboat from one side of the river to the other. The rope was tied around two big trees, on either side of the river. Her father had to put blinders on the horses to keep them quiet.

When they reached the house of her uncle, her father left her there for about a month until he returned for his next trade trip in Baiasa.

Thiana liked the big, stone house with tall, airy rooms, the great back yard full of chickens, the pork's pen and the cow, the pantries well stocked with cheese, eggs and butter.

While there, she heard stories about Migdala, the oldest of the girls, who was in love with a Greek man. Migdala was a beautiful young woman with long, dark hair that she braided in two thick braids that hung down her back down to her waist. She had black, shining eyes and was tall and slender. Her father had forbidden her to see the Greek man, or to marry him. So, Migdala would wake up during the night and sneak out of the house to meet her boyfriend. One cold, rainy night, when she went out to meet her man, she caught pneumonia. There were no medications for pneumonia except aspirin, and so her pneumonia degenerated into tuberculosis.

Thiana heard her aunt talking, "We've kept Thiana here for a month. We'll see if she remembers this, later."

When her father came back to pick up Thiana, the family sent their oldest daughter, Migdala, with them, to spend the summer at the high altitude of Avdela in the hope that the mountain air would improve her condition. They sent their daughter with presents for their relatives—whole wheels of cheese and butter.

When they arrived at their house in Avdela and Calliope heard the girl coughing all night, the very next morning she told her, "Look, I have five small children. I cannot keep you here for them to catch tuberculosis from you. It's contagious. You have to go back to your mother."

She sent the poor girl back.

Later they heard she had died.

chapter 6

Iani

Thiana's father, Iani, had no formal education, but he knew that in order for his children to have a better life than himself, they should go to school. He insisted that the oldest son, Take, and all others went to school. In Iani's opinion, as well as his wife's and the entire community, it was not as important for girls to go to school as it was for the boys. Girls were supposed to get married and take care of their families. And that was the case with Maritza, who mostly helped her mother with the chores around the house. Thiana went to the primary school in Grevena, the Greek School, and then, to the Intermediate school. That was all the formal education they expected her to get.

With Take, it was a different story. He was the pride of his parents and of all Avdela. Take was a good student. He took school seriously and intended to go further to high school and college to become a judge.

That was also the dream of his father.

Iani was a smart man. He understood that he was sick.

"Listen, I know I'm sick. My kidneys are failing," Iani said to his wife one morning.

"And how do you know?" Calliope asked. She'd noticed her husband's health failing and his energy diminishing, but still, she hoped it would be a passing thing.

"I have problems urinating. I know something is wrong with my kidneys," Iani said.

"And what are you going to do about it?" Calliope asked.

"I'll go to Ioannina. They have a big hospital there. I'll see a doctor. Maybe I'll need surgery. I don't know."

Ioannina was a big, ancient city on the western side of Lake Ioannina.

"When are you going to leave?"

"In a week. I have to set up my business and I'll give you all the money, I have. I'll only take my horse with me. When I reach Ioannina, I'll sell the horse at the market and go to the hospital."

"And how you're going to come back from Ioannina if you sell the horse?"

"I'll find somebody who'll bring me back. Don't worry, and take good care of the children. Take is old enough now. He'll help you."

He took his farewell from his wife and children and went alone on horseback to have the surgery done. He never came back.

Calliope heard from people arriving from the town to Avdela that her husband had died. From then on, Calliope's life as a young woman ceased. She started to wear black clothes and to tie her long hair with a black kerchief.

She, too, had died with her husband back on the surgery table.

Calliope's life from now on would be only for her children. She had five young children to raise all by herself and she had no skills except working around the house.

Calliope and her oldest daughter, Maritza, bought wool from the market—the cheapest short wool—and dyed it at home, spun it and wove it into rugs. Calliope sold them at the local open market on Saturdays. They had a few handmade tools to aid them in the rug making like the big, wooden comb with its sharp teeth, the upper part gliding against the lower part, combing the wool, or the old, wooden loom that sat in the big room.

Calliope and Maritza first washed the wool at the river. They set it upon a big, flat stone at the water's edge and beat the dirt out of it with a big wooden spoon, let it dry, and dyed it in natural colors by boiling it over an open fire in big cooper vases set outside in the front yard. Then, they spun it and wove it in rugs of vivid colors and intricate design.

They rented out the big house in Grevena and all six of them lived in the small cottage in the back yard during the winter months. In the summer, they lived in Avdela.

There, they had their vegetable garden that Calliope and Maritza tended.

Take took a job helping with calligraphy and book keeping at the village's office.

They barely made it, but they were happy. They had each other, and they didn't expect much.

Overnight, Take became the man of the house—a big job for his narrow shoulders.

When Take started to earn some money at his office job, sometimes he bought a small piece of meat and carried it in his hand so that everybody could see that his family was having meat for dinner. He would come proudly from the market, located on the *misimera*, the *platia* downtown, all the way to their house up on the hill with the meat in his hand.

One Easter, as Thiana remembered, Take brought home material for dresses for the girls. It was a green velvet—*catifee*—with small, pink flowers and Maritza, who learned to sew from her aunt, Kiaua, made new dresses for them to wear to Church.

One afternoon, Thiana and her four-year-old brother, Vangheli, a small, barefooted child wearing oversized pants passed down from his older brothers, were at their aunt Kiaua's house. Kiaua had her sewing machine set up in the great room. She was working at Thiana's catifee dress, her head bent down. The "Singer" machine was set up on a table, Kiaua's hands moving deftly, maneuvering the hand wheel of the machine, and the dress.

"Vangheli, leave that spool alone," Kiaua said, raising her head. She was beautiful with her chestnut hair tightly arranged around her smiling face.

"I didn't do anything," Vangheli was quick to defend himself. "The spool fell down and I was trying to retrieve it for you."

"Is that so. Then, give it to me."

Thiana was sitting quiet in a corner of the room, watching the scene. She noticed Vangheli smoothly pushing the spool of tread that fell from Kiaua's table with his bare foot, hiding it behind the open door. He hoped that Kiaua didn't see him.

"They could use a spool of thread at home," Thiana thought and said nothing.

chapter 7

The Easter Picnic

At Easter time, Thiana's mother, Calliope, was cooking *pita* with sugar and ground cinnamon without the pecans or much olive oil like the rich people did. They took it with them to the Easter picnic on Sunday morning. There they would sit by their richer cousins and were content.

At those picnics, the entire community would come with their Easter baskets full of food and would set up the *trapezumandeles*, the tablecloths, on the ground and the local gypsies would come and sing with their violins, at the request of the richest men. The young men and women would dance.

It was always a competition among men as to who could get the gypsies to play for them. The richest man and the proudest one would stick a bill on the gypsy's forehead and they would approach him where he was sitting on the ground and sing his request.

Beciu, the village butcher, a young ugly man with short bowed legs and mean squinty eyes, tried to get the gypsies to come over to where he was sitting and sing for him. He had his eye on Kiaua, Calliope's youngest sister, who was tall and beautiful.

Kiaua, like Calliope, walked tall and proud with her head held high. That in itself was a challenge to all men in Avdela.

The gypsies went to another man who paid them more money, and sang for him, as he danced with Kiaua.

Without much thought, Beciu took out his knife and cut the other man down. Thiana saw the blade of the pocketknife like lightning when Beciu took it out and thrust it with all his power into the other man's back as he was still dancing with Kiaua. It happened in a split second in the middle of the dance clearing with everybody watching. Blood gushed out of the man's mouth and back and he fell to the ground dead.

Kiaua screamed and ran as fast as she could and barricaded herself in the house until the Police caught Beciu. She was secretly in love with the other man and terribly afraid of Beciu.

Beciu went to prison for a while and then they let him free.

Killing was not uncommon in Avdela. Another Easter picnic, Thiana remembered, one of the young unmarried men of the community came and asked one of the married women to dance with him and when the dance had finished he kissed the woman on the mouth in front of her husband. He was obviously in love with the young woman and challenged the husband in front of the entire community. The husband stood up, took out his pocketknife and stabbed the young man in his belly, killing him on the spot.

The man remained unpunished.

According to the community's unwritten rules, he'd done nothing wrong.

He'd only defended his honor.

Chapter 8

Thana, The Mail Bride

Calliope had a brother, Nicolae, or Kulusu, as they called him, and four sisters, all tall, beautiful girls. The most beautiful of all of them was the oldest, Thana. Thana was tall and supple, willowy with long, chestnut hair and a white, creamy complexion. Thana was very delicate and sensitive—different from all the others.

Over times, some of the most daring men from Avdela, or the ones that had problems with the authorities, went to America to work and became rich. The Armani were always considered a partly nomadic people who liked to travel to new places. Like gypsies, they were at home all over the World. They were adventurous people with a lot of courage and determination.

It seems that almost all families from Avdela had a member who at one time left for America. America was the ultimate dream. The freedom. The country of opportunities.

The single men were the ones who often left for America and they worked hard to establish themselves, usually in restaurants. After that, they sent word back home that they were looking for a bride to come and join them in America. The word of mouth went by and usually the most beautiful girls were picked up as mail order brides.

Kulusu, Calliope's brother, went to America, but could not survive there. Either he was not willing to work that hard or apply himself, or he was not strong enough for manual labor. Kulusu returned to Avdela without becoming rich in America. Thiana remembered Kulusu's return to Avdela. The cambara rang and the entire village gathered in the misimera. Kulusu had returned from America. He wore a tall, black hat and striped pants and a black jacket with tails. He balanced a big umbrella in his hand, using it as a cane. The village people looked on with awe: "He must be rich. Look at his clothes. Look at his hat. Look at his umbrella. He probably returned rich."

As a rich-looking gesture, Kulusu threw away the big umbrella with a theatrical gesture, saying, "He was too rich now. He could discharge a good umbrella."

With the money he gained in America, Kulusu bought candles and sold them in Avdela and the nearby villages. The candles didn't sell, as he expected and Kulusu lost all his money.

But he also came back with the precise demand from an American-Arman to send him the most beautiful girl in Avdela for a bride. The man was established in New York and his family owned a restaurant. They were rich by everybody's standards. The way a man looked, or what his character was like, did not interest anybody. He was rich. That was all that counted. He ordered the most beautiful girl from Avdela. He would send her the ship ticket.

Now, the most beautiful girl in all Avdela was Thana and Kulusu picked her up to be the mail order bride.

People considered her lucky to be picked.

Or maybe Kulusu, her brother, had picked her with the secret desire that he'd go with her back to America and maybe he'd be allowed to work in his brother in law's restaurant.

After all the preparations were made and the bride was ready to leave, only one ticket arrived in the mail for Thana, and not a second one for Kulusu.

Thiana remembered how the entire family went with the bride to Salonika to bid her farewell. She was so beautiful, and so frail, so delicate, and so scared for what was waiting for her in America. Would she be able to cope with it all, without any of her own relatives close by? Did anybody care how she felt? Did anybody asked her if she preferred to stay home in Avdela and marry a man from home? Did anybody care that she might be too fragile to outstay the great adversities of an unknown place and unknown people? It was all Kulusu's making, in hope that he would return to America with her. And now, he would not be allowed to return. She would have to go alone.

Chapter 9

Kiaua

Kiaua, Calliope's youngest sister, was the only one who wasn't married. It was Beciu who'd courted her and wanted to take her for his wife. Everybody was afraid of Beciu and knowing he had his sights set on Kiaua no other man in the community dared to look at her.

Kiaua was terrified at the prospect of marrying Beciu and when she heard that Beciu was released from prison, in order to escape his unwanted attention, she left Avdela and the closed community and went with her brother, Kulusu, to Romania.

There, she rented a small apartment in the commercial center of Bucharest and established herself as a seamstress. Later, she found a man to her liking and married him.

In early 1930s, Thiana finished the Greek Intermediate School in Grevena. She was fourteen years old and restless. She wanted to see the world. In her own way, she was adventurous. She liked the unknown. She was not like her sister, Maritza, who took over the household chores and was happy to do it. She desired a better life for herself and her brothers and sister.

Thiana knew that there, in Avdela, she could not expect a better life.

* * *

Thiana decided to join her aunt, Kiaua, in Romania. There were her first cousins, from her father's side of the family, the Zarmans, who also lived in Romania. The word got back to Avdela that life in Romania was easier; Romania was a rich country, and its people very hospitable and kind.

Her mother was not opposed to the idea of Thiana leaving. She had her hands full with the younger children.

Until that time, Thiana was running the paths of Avdela barefoot and had never seen a car in her life.

Alexandru Zarman—Alexandrulea—as the relatives fondly called him, her first cousin, was married and established in Romania. He came and took Thiana with him back to Romania.

Thiana remembered her sister, Maritza, giving her a new pink coat for the trip. That and a small bundle of cloths were all the belongings she had.

Alexandrulea took her by hand and they left for Romania.

They rode the train from Grevena to Salonika and there embarked on a ship to Romania.

The ship, as Thiana remembered, stopped in Constantinople. There they visited the great Church, Aghia Sofia.

Thiana remembered the beautiful Turkish women, dancing in Constantinople, with their exposed bellies, undulating to the rhythm of the castanets, wearing sheer veils over their faces and long, sheer, bouffant pants, their feet bare.

The final destination for Thiana and Alexandrulea was Constantia, the Romanian port, at the Black Sea.

For Thiana it was all like a dream.

Chapter 10

Turtukoaia

When they arrived in Bucharest, the capital city of Romania, Alexandrulea took Thiana directly to her aunt, Kiaua. Kiaua rented a small apartment on "Calea Rahovey," the industrial/commercial center of Bucharest. Thiana gazed with awe at the narrow, cobblestone-paved streets and at the big, red brick buildings aligning the part commercial, part residential neighborhood. She marveled at the tram, quietly circulating, at the crowds of people milling on the streets, and at the cars driving through the narrow streets.

Kiaua was single and made her living as a seamstress. Her apartment was located on the second floor of a red brick building with an exterior stairway. Kiaua lived in the apartment upstairs and Kulusu, her brother, in the apartment downstairs.

Alexandrulea and Thiana climbed the stairway and knocked on the upstairs apartment door. Kiaua looked through the peephole and cracked the door a little bit.

"What do you want?" she asked. She was even more beautiful than Thiana remembered her: tall, slender and with her chestnut hair well arranged. She wore an elegant brown dress—nothing like the dresses she used to wear back in Avdela.

Alexandrulea pointed to Thiana, a small girl in a pink coat with a bundle in her hand. He said, "Here's your niece, Thiana, the daughter of your sister, Calliope, who came from Greece to live with you."

Kiaua stared at the little girl. "You brought her here, you take care of her. I don't want to have anything to do with her." She slammed the door shut in front of their faces.

Alexandrulea could not believe what was happening.

Thiana started to cry, not knowing what to do or say. What was to happen to her now?

"Don't cry, Thiana! And don't worry. I'm taking you to my home, to my wife, Lucica. She'll be happy to have you."

"But why? What did I do to her to throw me out like that? It was as if she didn't know me."

"It's not you. That's what life has done to her. You know, she practically had to run out of Avdela and her house there to escape Beciu and his unwanted attention toward her."

"I know that. I had been there, when Beciu killed the man she loved. But, that doesn't justify her behavior toward me. I'm her niece!"

"It's not about you. Life has hardened her heart. Too bad. Such a beautiful girl. Such a young woman."

Alexandrulea took Thiana with him to his house. It was located in a nicer neighborhood, Cotroceni, with nice residential houses on neat streets lined with old trees.

Alexandrulea was married to a nice, Jewish lady named Lucica. They had a big home, a maid, and a cook. They had two children of their own, Mara and Sotiris. Lucica received Thiana with open arms and treated her as one of her own children. Mara and Sotiris had a *freuland,* who spoke to them in German. Every week, a chariot full of provisions from their country house in Turtukoaia came over and brought to their residence big, smoked hams, chickens, fresh eggs, fruits, and vegetables.

In the fall, Alexandrulea enrolled Thiana in a girl's boarding school, "Pitarmosi," where she learned the Romanian language and studied to become a teacher. The school was run by nuns.

Thiana made friends with girls her age.

In the summer, when school was closed and everybody went on vacation to their homes, Alexandrulea took Thiana to her aunt Kiaua, to spend the summer months with her. Kiaua again refused to take the girl with her.

Alexandrulea took Thiana with him and his family to their family's vacation home, in Turtukoaia for the summer.

Thiana could not have asked for more. She loved Lucica and her girl. Their house in Turtukoaia was big and beautiful. The countryside was beautiful, too. Thiana remembered her first ball. Lucica's daughter, Mara, was a little bit older than she was and Lucica had given her a great ball.

Lucica gave Thiana a beautiful, new, long dress to wear. She arranged her hair up and wove flowers through it. Thiana sat on a chair next to the wall and watched the couples dancing on the dance floor. At midnight, the girls were back in their room and as the tradition was, they heated lead in a tablespoon over the open flame of a candle and poured hot, liquid lead in a glass of water and looked at the shape the lead took, dreaming of their future husbands.

In the morning, all the guests were invited on a trip with carriages and horses.

It was a beautiful time in Thiana's life.

Chapter 11

Salonika

While in Romania, Thiana grew up and blossomed. She was a beautiful, young woman with soulful, velvet-brown eyes and thick, light brown hair that she wore tightly arranged around her face. Like all women from her mother's side of the family, she held herself proudly and walked with her head held high. She learned the Romanian language and studied to become a teacher. She made good friends in school, at "Pitarmosi", friends she would have for her entire life, like Virginica and her sister, Margareta, two country girls who came to the capital to become teachers.

When she graduated from school, she was offered a position as a teacher at the Romanian Schools in Salonika, Greece.

"Now," Thiana thought, "she would go back to Greece and live there with her family. She had an education and a good salary. She would be able to help her family and live the life she desired."

Her family was established in Salonika. Her oldest brother Take became a judge, as her father wanted him to be. They all still lived together. Take helped his younger brothers through school. Toli, who was a bright student like Take once was, finished high school and decided to go to Italy to study to became a veterinarian. Maritza, Take, and Vangheli, the youngest brother, lived together with their mother, in a two-story house. Take became a judge in Kilkisa, a small town close to Salonika, and took care of them all.

Thiana left all her belongings to her aunt Kiaua in Bucharest—everything she'd acquired during her school years. She was her only relative, regardless of how Kiaua treated her.

It was the late 1930s when Thiana embarked on what she thought would be her last trip to her homeland. She took the train from Bucharest through Yugoslavia to Greece. In Yugoslavia, at Belgrade, the soldiers evacuated the train to search all the passengers for their papers. They took their time with Thiana's papers. By the time they were finished with her papers and ready to let her go, her train had already left the station. She was dressed for the big trip in a new pink suit and hat with high-heeled shoes. It was getting dark outside and the train station was closing for the night. The guard escorted her outside the station. Rain fell in straight curtains from the short awning of the building. Her pink suit was getting wet. "Where was she supposed to spend the night until the next morning when she could take the next train to Greece?" Thiana thought.

"Do you want to go with me to my house for the night?" A taxi stopped short in front of her and the man inside asked her in fluent Romanian.

"If you think that's O.K., maybe I'll go with you."

"You have nothing to worry about. I can assure you of that. I'll bring you back in the morning for your train."

The man took her to his house and offered her a chair next to the door to spend the night in. He went inside his bedroom.

Crunched in her chair, Thiana could hear him snore. She did not close her eyes all night long. In the morning, the man woke up and took her to the train station. He did not ask her for any money.

When she arrived in Salonika, she went straight to her family's house. She had sent them telegrams from Bucharest and then again from Belgrade about her arrival.

"*Qui,* is that you Thiana? I didn't recognize you! How beautiful you are. And how elegant you are! Come inside, let the others look at you!" Her mother greeted her at the doorway.

"Mother, I missed you all so much. I'm so glad to be home. Maritza how are you? Vangheli, you really grew up. You're a man now!"

She could not contain her joy of being reunited with them at last.

"I brought you all presents. Let's open my suitcases and I'll give them to you. You have a nice house here. Where is Take?"

"Take lives in Kilkisa. He's a judge there. He'll be here tomorrow to see you. You know, Take is renting this big house for us, so we can live here near him," her mother said with pride.

Thiana could see it. Take was still her favorite son. She was very proud of him.

"What about the house in Avdela? Do you still have it?" Thiana asked.

"Of course, we kept it, but we sold though the house in Grevena," her mother said.

Thiana came home a young, sophisticated lady. She no longer was the small girl running around in her bare feet. She had a good job and made good money.

The first thing Thiana did with her money was to buy a dowry for her older sister, Maritza, so she could get married. At that time in Greece, the requirement for a girl to get married was to have dowry. With a big dowry, she'd have a better choice of husbands.

Thiana put all her salary aside and bought Maritza everything—the entire trousseau. Maritza married a simple boy from Avdela and was happy.

Thiana was free to think about her and what she wanted out of life. She knew she'd liked to have nice, elegant dresses and shoes and have her hair done and to wear beautiful modern hats. She also had places to go and wear all those things. She was going to the school elegantly dressed.

The Romania School in Salonika was a conglomerate of old, sturdy buildings located in the best neighborhood of Salonika. It was a community within itself. It had classrooms and administrative buildings and had its own cafeteria and kitchen and well-stocked pantries. It was run by Romanian teachers managed by their Director.

Thiana met the other teachers, all of them, and had set her eyes on the Director of the School, a handsome, sophisticated man, a few years her senior.

He was Romanian.

Chapter 12

Costin

Costin was a bachelor at that time with no intention of marrying. Not now, not maybe ever. He had too good a time being the most eligible bachelor in Salonika. The Romanian Government had sent him to Greece and to Salonika to establish the first Romanian schools in Greece. He had absolute control over the school and its organization and finances. He was a graduate of the High Academy of Commerce back in Bucharest and was an expert in finance. He was also an accomplished teacher. He loved children and believed in higher education.

Costin had a lot of friends. All the other professors at the school were his friends. He never learned the Greek language, because he lived among Romanians at the school. The school was organized to be self-sufficient. The teachers had their own dormitories near the dormitories for the students, if they wanted to live on campus.

However, Costin and his friends enjoyed going out almost every night at the elegant restaurants on the seashore. Who needed a wife and the nagging that goes along with marriage, when beautiful women and accomplished colleagues were fighting for his time and attention?

Every evening, a different teacher gave a private party at his house and all the others attended.

At the time, Costin lived in a rented house. He had a housekeeper, who also cooked on occasion. Not that he didn't know how to cook. He was raised, as he liked to brag, in his mother's kitchen. He knew how to cook and present a meal if he had to do it. For now, there were too many women willing to do that for him.

Costin liked a good time and a drink. He came from the northeast part of Romania in Moldova where people enjoyed a glass of good wine and good food over leisurely conversations.

He had the school and the children to think of.

Costin was raised and educated to be a perfect gentleman. He knew how to treat a woman, how to be courteous and gallant.

chapter 13

The Courtship

Thiana was going to meet one of her new colleagues for lunch. She wore an elegant, gray, two-piece suit, with a matching hat and high-heeled shoes. She knew she looked her best.

She was stepping down from the bus, when she saw Costin approaching. He was a strong handsome in his early forties with a high forehead and shining, brown eyes beneath thick brows. He wore an elegant, off-white silk suit and a broad-rimmed Panama hat. He was the epitome of elegance, exuding self-confidence and charm.

Thiana hesitated and gazed up at him as he came toward her. She was not sure he remembered her from school.

After all, she was the youngest teacher and always sat at the far end of the table, when they had a teacher's meeting in the school's conference room. She never spoke up and nobody paid any attention to her.

He came toward her and said in his most gallant tone, "Good morning, madam! How are you?"

Thiana was astonished that he addressed her at all.

"I'm fine, thank you. My name is Thiana, in case you don't remember."

"Yes, I remember. Of course. How are you?" He repeated.

It was obvious to Thiana that he didn't remember her.

"Well since we already know each other, would you like to join me for lunch?"

"I'll like that," Thiana answered without hesitation.

She totally forgot about her previous engagement.

They started dating. Costin took her to the elegant restaurants located along the seashore in the evenings. They met their colleagues and had long dinners and discussions over gourmet meals and glasses of good wine. The band played soft music and they danced.

The gypsy violinist would come to their table and Costin would request the most beautiful Romanian love songs just for her. The young gypsy girls approached the table, with fresh cut flowers and Costin bought her violets.

Evenings they strolled on the promenade along the seashore hand-in-hand.

Thiana wanted a commitment. She wanted a family and a husband to stand by her side all her life.

She decided to take matters in her own hands. They were having dinner alone at a secluded restaurant on the seashore.

"I would like to get married," she said, in a matter-of-fact voice.

"That's nice. I personally do not intend to marry! Ever. I'm very happy the way I am. I enjoy my life, just the way it is. I don't need to get married," Costin answered.

He was astonished by her demands. Such things didn't happen in his world. A woman did not propose to a man. And she didn't propose—she demanded it! He laughed in her face.

Thiana was not accustomed to such treatment. She had built up her life all on her own. She'd fought life's hardships and won. She knew who she was. When Costin laughed, she responded, "Then you're not capable of getting married".

Costin shrugged his shoulders and laughed, "The little woman has some nerve."

Not long after that they were married.

Chapter 14

Olga

It was the year of 1938. The beginning of the end. Europe was on the brink of the Second World War and didn't yet know it.

Everywhere in Europe people partied and were having a good time. They ignored the imminent danger, the dark clouds gathering over their heads in the European skies.

It was the same for Bucharest, Romania.

Elegant people, negligently spending their money and their time enjoying the evenings and nights in elegant restaurants drinking, eating, dancing, and listening to music.

Costin wanted to have his wedding in Bucharest so that his sisters and brothers could attend the ceremony.

Thiana and Costin left Salonika by airplane and flew to Bucharest.

* * *

There, he took his bride to be and introduced her to his family—his sister Olga, and his brother Costica, the Navy Commander, and Gorg, his older brother.

They stayed in the apartment Costin owned on Maria Rosetti, a secluded neighborhood located in close proximity of the University. The apartment was a flat situated on the fifth floor of an old, elegant, apartment building. The apartment had three bedrooms, a living room, a dining room, and a study with hard wood floors and glass french doors that opened from the study and the master bedroom toward a wide balcony wrapped around the front of the building. The spare furniture was what Costin had owned as a bachelor: a big yellow bed and an armoire in the master bedroom, a square oak table occupying the dining room, a solid pecan wood desk with a green felt top, his pride.

Thiana felt claustrophobic about living in the small rooms of the apartment, and didn't like being on the fifth floor of a tall building. She missed the outdoors. For now, the apartment would have to do. She had every intention of buying a house later on, a house with ample ground around it, so she could breathe again.

Costin's younger brother, Costica, was a Commander in the Navy and also lived in Bucharest. Costin's younger sister, Olga, worked at the Telephone Company in Bucharest. Neither Olga nor Costica were married. Costin's older brother, Gorg, lived in Ploiesti, an industrial town located about 60 km north of Bucharest. Gorg was married to Janet and they lived in a small house with a garden located on the outskirts of Ploiesti. Costin's older sister, Maria, lived in the family home in Focsani, in Moldova, and was married.

* * *

Thiana and Costin met Costin's younger sister, Olga, at the fashionable brewery "Carul cu Bere" in the center of Bucharest behind Calea Victoriei. Thiana looked on in awe at the old, large room with its vaulted ceiling and wood beams, oil murals, and huge crystal chandeliers. Elegant people occupied the tables, each set with cream colored linen.

Olga came into the restaurant. She was tall, beautiful, and even a little taller than Costin, Thiana thought, elegantly dressed in an expensive pinstriped suit with a silver fox tossed across her shoulders and an eccentric hat on her head.

"You look positively beautiful," Costin greeted his sister. "Please, have a seat and I'll introduce you to my fiancée, Thiana. Thiana, this is my baby sister, Olga."

Thiana was intimidated by the poised, beautiful woman.

"Thiana is originally from Greece. Her family lives in Salonika where my school is. She is a teacher at the school where I'm the director."

"Does she speak any Romanian?" Olga asked with a high demeanor.

"Of course, she speaks Romanian. She was educated here in the country. She is a teacher at the Romanian school."

"Well, that's very nice. Did you hear, I'm also engaged to be married?" Olga made the transition quickly, shifting the attention to her. "I'm going to have some pate and a glass of beer," she said to the waiter who had been hovering around.

"That's good! We'll have the same," Costin said to the waiter. "Yes, I've heard that," he turned his full attention back to Olga. Which of the Dinescu brothers are you going to marry? You know, I went to school with one of them."

"No. He's not the one who was at the Academy with you. He's the youngest brother. We call him Mitica."

"And what's Mitica doing?"

"He's an accountant with a vineyard company in Focsani."

"So, we're going to move back to Focsani pretty soon, then."

"As soon as we get married."

"How is Maria?"

"She's fine. She sends her best wishes for your wedding. Where do you plan to have it?"

"We're thinking to talk to Costica to have it at the 'Casa Armatei.'"

"Yes. That sounds good. I'll wear a long dress, then."

chapter 15

The Engagement Party

Thiana met Costin's younger brother, Costica, the Navy Commander, at the Casa Armatei, the Army/Navy Club, a monumental ornate building located at the corner of Calea Victoriei and Regina Elisabeta Boulevard. They were having lunch. Thiana dressed for the occasion in her forest green suit and her beige felt hat. She wore her small red foxes around her neck. She knew the well-cut suit and her high-heeled suede pumps were showing off her slender, petite silhouette. The air was cooling with the fast approach of the fall. Elegant women, hanging at the arms of uniformed men were climbing the wide, granite stairs toward the restaurant.

In front of the restaurant's entrance there was a large outside terrace set with small round tables and umbrellas. Thiana saw a very tall man, dressed in his navy uniform, his spine a straight arrow, approaching their table.

"This is Costica, 'the Commander,'" Costin said.

"Hi! I apologize for being late," Costica said, in the most formal voice.

"This is my fiancée, Thiana."

"Nice to meet you. Olga told me about meeting you," Costica said and gallantly kissed Thiana's hand.

"He looks like a shining prince from a movie," Thiana thought, eyes glued to the handsome man's face. "He is much taller than Costin, and what an authoritative demeanor," she thought. She turned her eyes toward Costin. Her heart skipped a beat. With his gray suit, narrow silk tie, and the wide-brimmed, felt hat tipped above one eyebrow, he was definitely her prince charming. His kind eyes and gallant manner had stolen her heart.

"We wanted to ask you if it was possible for you to help us arrange so that we could have our wedding Casa Armatei," Costin said.

"It will be my pleasure to arrange it," Costica answered.

He was well known there and as Thiana had heard, Costica had earned the highest military honor, "The Cross of Mihai Viteazu," by saving his ship and his men in battle with the Russians.

Thiana brought all of them presents. She wanted her future husband's relatives to like her and receive her as a member of their family. Instinctively, she knew that Costin, even though he didn't talk much about it, loved his family very much.

She loved Costin and wanted to be accepted by his family.

She gave Olga the gold and silver belt she bought in Sofia on her last trip. It was an intricate hand-worked filigree belt, with alternate gold and silver segments.

Olga accepted it as if she deserved it, or it was something that Thiana had to do in order to buy her favors.

Olga really looked down upon Thiana. Thiana loved Costin and wanted to be with him, so she did not say anything.

They went to the City Hall located in "Piatza Amzei" and tried to apply for a marriage license. There, they received a shock. Thiana was a Greek Citizen. Costin was a Romanian Citizen. They could not be married in Romania.

They would have to wait to go back to Greece to be married.

They still could be engaged, though.

Thiana, with Costica's help, planned the engagement party at the "Army House." It was by far the most elegant club in Bucharest. Great, crystal chandeliers lighted the great ballrooms and the hard wood floors were highly polished. Heavy, oriental rugs covered the floors of the smaller dining rooms and card rooms.

Thiana ordered a long, slim, purple dress for herself. It had a slit in the back down to her waist and it showed off her perfect, petite figure. She wore it with high-heeled black, suede pumps. She had small, white, heavy-scented flowers braided into her thick, chestnut hair.

Her big brown eyes were shining. Her big day was here. She was engaged to be married to her prince, to the man of her dreams and nothing, nothing could get between them from now on. Not his relatives, or hers.

Chapter 16

Salonika II

It was 1943 and World War II was in full swing. Countries in Europe were taking sides.

Thiana watched as the German Army marched into the streets of Salonika; how they installed their camps around town; how they gradually took over everything. Everyone was under suspicion. At night, in the restaurants, German officers talked loudly and took over, disrupting the music and dance. On the streets after dark, the German soldiers checked everyone. The persecution against Jews had begun. They were rounded up in Platia Aristotle's in the middle of town one-by-one; no one knew, how they found out their names. They were stripped of their clothing and flogged in the middle of the day in plain view of the crowds. They were branded and sent away, each one with a small bundle in their hands, old people and young people and children. Nobody knew, exactly, where they were taken or why.

Thiana always thought how ironic it was that the city's landmark, the "White Tower," the 15th century Venetian circular tower, now a museum, was used by the Ottomans as a place for the execution of janissaries, which is why it was known as the "Tower of Blood." "History repeats itself," Thiana thought.

Thiana witnessed as the Germans soldiers executed an entire village. The water reservoir for the entire town was located in a small village, Horiatis, just outside Salonika. The Germans had soldiers there around the clock guarding the potable water supply. One dark night, people from the village killed the German guard near the water reservoir and threw his dead body into the reservoir. The very next day, Thiana witnessed as the Germans soldiers called out all the people from the village, rounded them up in Platia Aristotle's in a circle and shot all of them. Then, they burned the entire village. They'd done it so that everybody could take notes and witness that nobody could kill a German soldier and remained unpunished.

There was a story of a young Jewish girl who was a clerk at the local grocery store. The family who owned the store thought of her as one of them. They hid her in the basement and kept her there until the war was over. The young, beautiful girl came out of the basement years later with all her hair white, an old woman, and remained unmarried all her life with the family who had saved her life. She would not talk to anybody, doing her chores solemnly day after day, oblivious to anyone around her. In her mind, she remained in the dark basement for the rest of her life.

There was the old Jewish man who lived downstairs at *Kiria*, or Madame Marika, in the same rented house where Thiana and Costin had lived, who was taken away by the Germans and sent to "Auschwitz." He returned when the war was over to the same house. He called Thiana downstairs and showed her a case of jewelry he had hidden in the basement of the house before the war.

* * *

Thiana's family lived together and Costin moved in with them for the time being.

Thiana was pregnant with her first child, approaching her ninth month of pregnancy.

In Salonika and at the Romanian school there, everything was still under control. People went about their business as usual with certain restrictions and inconveniences. Nobody realized the imminent danger.

They were not yet affected personally.

Chapter 17

Tirgoviste

In August of 1944, Thiana and Costin were in Bucharest visiting with Costin's Family. Costin wanted his first child, hopefully a boy, be born in his own country, Romania close to his family.

Overnight, the war came to Romania. The Russian Army moved forward west and pushed the German Army out of every country they passed through. The Allied forces bombarded Bucharest.

Everybody in Bucharest moved outside of the capital to the small towns in the country. They thought they would to be safer. They thought the Capital was going to be heavily bombarded.

Thiana and Costin went to a small town at the toe of the Carpatin Mountains— Tirgoviste. At the end of August, Costin had to go to Salonika to the school to pay the teachers' salaries. At the time he had an airplane at his discretion and thought he'd only be gone a day. He told Thiana to stay at the hotel in Tirgoviste and await his return.

It was a luxurious hotel and Tirgoviste was a quiet, little town, about two hour's drive outside Bucharest. He thought Thiana would be safe there until he returned.

He never got a chance to do so.

War was declared overnight. All communications between Romania and Greece ceased.

Chapter 18

The Hospital

Thiana found herself suddenly in the middle of the war. The bombs came down on Tirgoviste and people were evacuated from the hotel.

"We're sorry for the inconvenience, but you might have to leave the hotel room and go downstairs into the basement. The hotel might be bombed," a young bellboy tried to tell her when she answered the doorbell in the middle of the night.

"But why, what happened?" Thiana asked, panic sinking in.

"We are at war. War has been declared. We heard the announcement over the radio on the eleven o'clock news. A state of emergency has been declared in the country. The King addressed the nation at eleven o'clock last night. The hotel's management wants all their guests in the basement for tonight, just to be safe."

After the bellboy left, Thiana ran toward the phone and tried to call Costin's brother, Costica, in Bucharest. If any one should know about the war, Costica would know. He was an active officer, in the Royal Navy.

The telephone's tone was a continuous busy signal. She called time and time again. She wanted to calm down, so she put some clothes on over her night grown in case she had to leave quickly. She couldn't think straight. "What's going to happen to Costin, in Greece? Was he all right? She must reach Costica and talk to him, no matter what. Who else could she call? The hotel reception offered only polite excuses, empty words. She felt trapped in the luxurious hotel room all by her self. She had nobody to call upon. Nobody to talk to. Nobody to ask advice. Should she pack her belongings? Would they let her stay in the hotel? Where would she go?"

She heard the alarm shrieking outside, people hurrying down the hallway, doors opening and closing, people talking and calling out to each other.

She lay on the bed. Her back hurt badly. She felt her first contraction and doubled over with pain. "What was she supposed to do?" The thought entered her mind, just for a fraction of a second, "Should she die in a bombing or in labor, nobody will ever know what happened." Then, resolutely, she pushed the thought out of her mind.

She forced herself to calm down. She had to think first of the new life ready to come out of her, her unborn child. She had to call the hotel management. Maybe somebody would drive her to the hospital. She needed to go to the hospital, right away. She'll try to call Costica later. Right now, she had to get to the hospital.

She rang the hotel management and begged for help getting to the hospital. The hotel manager sent a porter to take her down and put her into a cab. By the time they reached the hospital, her water had broken.

By then, the hospital was full of injured soldiers and civilians. Wounded people were everywhere: in the corridors, on the floors, in every bed. Nobody paid attention to her.

That night, she gave birth to her daughter, Magdalena, alone with a midwife in a hospital room. They put her in a bed in an empty room. The doctor came and looked at her for what seemed to be only a second: "You've started to dilate, already. Is this your first child?" he asked in a hurried tone.

"Yes," Thiana's voice was weak.

"I'll send a midwife to stay with you for the night. I'm busy with more important matters as you can see." He turned his back on her and left.

Contractions came increasingly often. The pain was unbearable. After each contraction, she felt weaker and weaker. What if something's wrong? At least, she could scream out, loud. Nobody paid attention to her.

"Please, somebody come over and help me. I'm in labor," she wailed in between her contractions.

Finally, a heavy woman came into the room. "Calm down now. We're going to be all right." She reached down and looked at her. "You're almost there. You're a strong woman. It will be a little while, now."

"Please, please, for God's sake, stay with me."

"I'll stay with you, don't worry. Just reach behind you and hold onto the bed's rails. And push, push as hard as you can."

It seemed to Thiana that the contractions were going on forever. Finally, she heard a small cry coming out from between her legs.

"Hey, you've done it! You have a beautiful daughter. Here, look for yourself. What will you name her?"

"What? Give me the child! She's beautiful. Costin will be disappointed. He wanted a son."

"Do you know what you'll name her? We need to register the birth here at the hospital."

"I don't know yet. We were hoping to have a son. I'll call her Magdalena. After Maria-Magdalena."

"Let me change the bed now, and your night gown. I'll put you in some nice, clean cloths. Don't fall asleep right the way. It's not good for you. You'll bleed to death. Try to stay awake for a while. I'll leave you and your daughter now. Feed her when you can."

Chapter 19

The Russian Soldier

The rumors were that the Russian Army was entering Tirgoviste on their way to Bucharest. People said that the Russians were barbarians. The soldiers raided every town and village on their way, stole valuables from the houses, and raped every woman left behind. Everybody hid or ran away.

Thiana had no place to hide and nowhere to run.

She stayed alone, holding her daughter tight at her breast in the now empty hospital. It had been evacuated overnight.

At least the midwife had changed her sheets and her night grown before she left. She also left her a jug of tea and some food on a plate on the nightstand next to her bed. The baby was wrapped in a clean sheet, sleeping peacefully. She just finished breast-feeding her. She was so tiny, so perfect.

She could hear heavy steps approaching in the hallway. The echo sounded sinister in the empty building. "The Russians are here. They might harm the baby and me. God, oh God, please, save my baby and me. Make them leave. Make them not enter my room. We'll stay quiet. Not a sound. God, please, let them leave my baby and me alone."

A Russian soldier opened the door. He looked rugged, like a barbarian with his dirty, blonde, overgrown hair and beard, big, dirty boots and dirty khaki uniform. His sleeves were rolled up and he wore several watches, on both arms.

He stopped in the doorway as if a bolt of lightning had struck him. He looked at her and the new born child at her breast.

"God bless you," he said in Russian, made the sign of cross and left, and closed the door behind him.

chapter 20

The Train

Thiana woke up feeling stronger. The deep sleep and the little food she had eaten the night before had helped her get her strength back. She looked down at the baby, sleeping next to her on the bed. She needed to get out of this empty place before more Russian soldiers showed up. She might not be so lucky next time.

Slowly, as if trying her strength, she got out of the bed and took a nice silk dress out of her suitcase. She spread the navy-blue dress over the bed and slowly walked to the sink in the corner of the room. She glanced at herself in the mirror above the sink. She looked shallow, with dark circles beneath her eyes. Her hair was a matted mess. She took the towel hanging from a hook next to the sink and cleaned herself as best she could. She went back to the bed, took the baby, and very careful cleaned her. Then, she wrapped the baby in one of her dresses. She combed her hair carefully. It has to do for now. There was no way; she could wash her hair with the cold water in the sink.

Now, she looked a little better. She put on the silk dress and wore flat sandals on her bare feet. She took her baby in one arm and her suitcase in the other.

She had to get to the train station. She had to catch a train to Bucharest to contact Costin's brother and sisters to find out news about Costin. When she reached the street, it looked deserted. There were no cabs around. She had to walk over to the train station.

The train was full of people leaving in a panic. It moved slowly and stopped at every station. People crowded one on top of the other in the corridors and inside the cabins, hanging from the train's platforms and stairs.

Thiana had nothing to eat from the night before, and it seemed now, to have been days since she'd eaten. Her stomach growled. The child needed nourishment. She was crowded in hallway of the train holding her baby tightly in her arms. Now that she was in the train and on her way, all her strength seemed to have left her and she felt dizzy. There was not enough air. People were too close all around her, suffocating her. She put her suitcase down. Who cared about the suitcase? She had to hold onto the baby. Her head was pounding. She did not have air. She started to say something, but no sound came out.

She did not remember when she fell down. It was so hot. She could not move, or open her eyes, but she could hear people around her talking:

"Does anybody know who she is?"

"Is she with anybody here?"

"If she dies, what's going to happened to the child?"

"Does anybody want to take the child?"

"Should we let the train conductor know about her?"

"Bring here some water. I'll try to revive her. Maybe, she will open her eyes."

Thiana could feel the man on top of her, slapping her face hard, first on one side, then on the other. Another man poured cold water on her. She could hear her baby crying beside her.

She made a supreme effort and opened her eyes. She did not want her child to grow up without knowing her mother or father.

"Now, you're coming around. Are you all right? Here, drink some water." A man was holding a bottle with water to her mouth with one arm, while the other held her head up. Thiana swallowed the lukewarm water.

"Thank you. I'm all right now. Where is my baby?"

"Your baby is here," a woman said, holding the baby in her thick arms.

"Give me my baby," Thiana said as she was helped to her feet. "I'm alright now."

She grabbed her baby from the other woman's arms.

"Here, eat this." The man who helped her to her feet held out a piece of bread. "You'll feel better. And here, come sit down on your suitcase."

"Thanks a lot. I have not eaten since last night." Thiana took the bread and slowly ate it.

Gradually, people around her returned to their own conversations and left her alone. They left her a little more space, so she could sit on her suitcase with her baby in her arms.

Chapter 21

Gorg

Finally, the train arrived to the North Train Station in Bucharest. Thiana waited until everybody left the train and then she climbed down with her baby held tight in her arms. She looked for a pay phone and called Costica at the Casa Armatei.

"Costica, this is Thiana. I just arrived in Bucharest, from Tirgoviste, by train."

"Well, I'm glad to hear from you. Last I knew you were in Tirgoviste, while Costin left for Greece. Are you all right?"

"I'm all right, now. And the baby too."

"Did you have your baby?" Costica could not believe his ears. "By yourself?"

"I was in the hospital, in Tirgoviste. They were evacuating the town and the hospital."

"Is the baby alright?"

"Yes. I have a beautiful girl. I named her Magdalena, after Maria-Magdalena. Did you hear from Costin?"

"No, not yet. As you probably heard, we are at war. All communications have ceased between Greece and the outside world. Where are you now? I'll come and pick you up."

"I'm at the North Train Station. I'll wait for you, here."

How comforting to know that somebody cared about her. That she was not alone in the world, after all.

Costica took Thiana and the newborn child, to his apartment. He had an apartment on the Splaiul Independent Street and an assistant at his command. The ordinance was a sailor, by the name of Ion, whose primary duty was to take care of Costica's needs.

Thiana and Costin's apartment on Maria Rosette had been rented out at the time and was occupied. She couldn't stay there.

Costica decided to move to the Officers' quarters and left Ion, the assistant, to take care of Thiana and the child in his apartment.

"Make yourself at home. And let Ion know if you need something. He would bring it for you," Costica said, as he walked out the front door.

Ion brought food and clothes for her and the baby from the Officers' quarters.

Later, Costin's younger sister, Olga, came by the apartment and took everything that was left there, leaving the house nearly empty. She was also expecting a child at the time and was jealous of her brother paying attention to his sister-in-law, instead of herself.

"You know those are really my things. I need them. As you could see for yourself, I'm expecting a child too," Olga said. "You're probably going back to Greece soon, aren't you?"

"Yes, of course. As soon as I'm able to travel and the baby puts some weight on. You're welcome to take whatever you like from here. It's Costica's house, after all, not mine," Thiana said.

Later, that day, Gorg, Costin's older brother, came by the apartment. He was an older gentleman and on the heavy side. Since Thiana had first met him, Gorg always had a kind smile and a good word for her. He came with a basket full of fresh fruits and vegetables from his garden.

"I'm happy to see you, Gorg. I'm happy you brought the fresh fruits and vegetables. My baby needs some nourishment."

"We're most welcome. Did you hear what Olga asked me to buy for her child?"

"No. What?"

"She asked me, to buy her a carrier."

"And what did you say?" Thiana asked.

"That she had a husband to buy her whatever she needs."

"That was good. She deserves it. She came by right before you and took the rugs. You remember the one that was handmade, which I knew belonged to Costin. She said they were hers. I didn't argue."

"She is only after what she could take. You know," Gorg, said, "that before I came here, I went to see Costica, at the Casa Armatei. Well, I went like this, with the bounder hanging on my arm. I thought I'd surprise him. What do you think, he said?"

"What?" Thiana asked, amused. Gorg was so gentle, so nice. He reminded her of her husband.

"He was ashamed of me. He didn't want his colleagues, the other officers, to know that I'm his brother."

"He's a snob, all right, but he has a golden heart. You and I both know it. He left me and my child here and he moved out immediately and brought me everything I needed from the officers' headquarters." Thiana felt better in the company of the kind man.

"You know how much I love, Janet, my wife. I thought, that I'd stay in Ploiesti, when they bombed the town and maybe I'd be lucky to find a silk parachute. Somebody could fall out of the sky with his parachute on and then I'd take it. It would make a nice blouse for Janet."

"Gorgusor," Thiana used the loving diminutive of his name, "that's such a nice thought." Thiana said, moved to tears by his obvious love toward his wife.

Janet was sick. Puss was coming out of a wound on her side next to her breast and the doctors could not heal the wound. Gorg was tenderly taking care of her.

Later, Gorg and Thiana went to the open market. He bought a small, wooden tub to bathe her little daughter in.

The child was sick and she was exhausted. Since she was born, the baby could not take nourishment well. She would throw up immediately after meals. Either the baby was sick, or she was too nervous and anxious and her milk was more like poison to the baby, instead of nourishment.

Besides her baby, all of Thiana's thoughts and worries were about Costin and her family in Greece.

chapter 22

The Freight Train

All communications with Greece had been severed. No passenger trains were leaving from Bucharest—not to Greece, or to anywhere.

Thiana could not stay still, not without knowing what had happened to Costin and her family. She had to go back to Greece. She just had to find a way.

She took her daughter in her arms and went to the North Train Station, located in the center of Bucharest, on Calea Grivitei, and waited for any train at all that was leaving from Bucharest. She wrapped Magdalena in a dark red duvet that Costin had given her. It reminded her of her husband and somehow gave her strength.

The only train leaving for Greece was a freight train carrying animals. She climbed unobserved onto the platform of an empty flatcar and waited for the train to leave.

She had no papers with her, just a bundle in her hand, her daughter in her arms, and the dress on her back.

The train moved at a snail's pace, stopping at every station for hours at a time and sometimes in the middle of the open fields. It took the train three whole days to reach Timisoara, the frontier point, to Yugoslavia. Luckily for her nobody noticed her.

The train reached Salonika, early in the morning. It was still dark outside.

Thiana jumped from the flatcar and in her bare feet. Her dress was torn and dirty, and her child needed changing. With her baby in her arms, she ran to her house to find Costin. The landlady of the house, Kiria Marika, came outside: "Is that you, Thiana? Are you looking for Costin? He doesn't come home very often these days. He's probably out, having a good time with his friends. You'd better go to your mother's house," the woman told her.

Thiana could not believe her ears. She ran in her bare feet with her daughter in her arms up the hill to her mother's house. The house was dark, with its windows closed and the shutters closed. She remembered now. It was war and the town was in camouflage. It was night and everybody was asleep, the house engulfed in darkness.

"Mother, it's me, Thiana. I came home!" Thiana screamed outside her mother's house.

"*Qui*! It's that you, Thiana? Her mother leaned out, of the second floor's window. Come inside. Vangheli go and get her."

Vangheli, her younger brother, who was all grown up, came out of the house. "Were you looking for Costin?"

"Yes, of course, I was looking for Costin," Thiana answered, panic rising in her voice.

"Well, he's out at the restaurant, drinking. He forgot about you and about us. He moved out of our house. We thought, you were never going to come back. Is this your child?"

"Yes. This is my daughter. I'm not coming inside the house until I find Costin. Take me to the restaurant where he is."

"O.K. I'll take you. Aren't you going to change your clothes, first?"

"I suppose I should." Thiana looked down at her torn, dirty, dress and her bare, dirty feet.

She went inside her mother's house.

"Do you have your passport and your papers in order? Take asked her as soon as she entered the room.

"No, I came on a freight train. It took me several days. I haven't eaten anything for days. I don't even have milk for the child anymore. It dried up. Who cares about the papers and the passport? I came alone. Nobody's seen me. I want to find Costin and let him know about our daughter. Vangheli, please take me to find Costin, now!"

"Look, you're going to put all of us in danger. Things have changed. You have to go back to the check point and let them mark your papers. After that, you can come back here and we'll find Costin for you. Now, you have to go back and report to the authorities. Vangheli, take her back, immediately!"

"I'm not supposed to even change, or clean up, or eat anything?" Thiana asked, not believing her own family.

"After they've checked you." Take did not bend.

Take, her older brother, was afraid of her coming with no papers in the middle of the night without the authorities knowing about her arrival. Take was a judge at the time and afraid of losing his job. He'd become a serious young man with his thick, brown hair all slicked back and glasses perched on his nose.

To her own family, she'd become the outsider, the enemy.

chapter 23

Gully al Spanou.

Vangheli escorted Thiana and her baby back to the frontier point. He was a youngster now, trying to look older than his age, with suspenders holding up his baggy pants and the sleeves of his white shirt rolled up to his elbows, his hair slicked back.

Thiana tried to sneak back into the building without being noticed by the guard. By the front door, crouched down, she noticed an old man mending his tethered shirt and singing softly.

"He's probably a beggar, or a crazy man," she thought, looking fearfully in his direction. Then, she recognized Gully al Spanou from Avdela. She was sure it was Gully al Spanou. But, what was he doing there, looking like a beggar and a fool? Everybody in Avdela knew he was the richest man around, with enough money to buy the entire village.

"Gully, it's that you? She approached the man and started speaking in Macedonian.

He slowly looked up at her, "*Qui*, my little girl! Do not say anything to anybody, about recognizing me! They'll kill me! Tell me what you need and I'll make sure you get it! Now, go quietly and *do not*, I repeat, *do not* tell anybody, including Costin, that you saw me!"

"That's very strange, Thiana thought, he recognized me and even knew to whom I was married."

"I'll do as he said. Maybe, he'll provide me with some strong, Russian tea for my daughter. She needs it for her stomach. Since we left Romania, she's been sick. Maybe he can help get some clean clothes for her. And maybe they'll let me go sooner if I tell him."

Gully made sure she got the tea for her daughter, clean clothes for her and her daughter and by next day, they let her go. She, on the other hand, kept her promise and did not tell anybody, about meeting him.

When she reached her mother's home the second time, still with the baby in her arms, she went in search of her husband. This time, she cleaned up and wore her beige silk dress and her brown, high-heeled suede pumps. She also cleaned and changed the child. She hadn't closed her eyes for several days, now. She was bone tired.

She found Costin at the restaurant. He'd grown a mustache and by the looks of it, he was having a good time with his friends.

Thiana went up at the table and showed him the child.

"I came back. This is our daughter."

He looked at her and the child and said: "Ah, here you are! I am glad you're back! Is this our girl?" He spoke as if she'd just stepped outside for a moment and now, she was back.

"Yes! This is Magdalena."

"Well, I'm glad you're here. Take a seat and let's celebrate your return and the birth of our daughter. What's her name?"

"Her name is Magdalena. You know, like Maria-Magdalena." Of course we must have to baptize her.

"That's nice, a nice name. Sit down. Would you like something to drink or eat?"

"Look, I came here to take you home with me. We have a lot of things to discuss," Thiana said with authority in her voice. Things were out of control. She needed to take charge of the situation.

"I cannot just go and leave my friends. We might have to stay a little and share the good company."

"I said we have to go home! I'm sure your friends will understand that you have not seen your wife and child in some time!"

"Let's go home, then." Reluctantly, Costin walked out with her on his arm.

He acted as if nothing was out of the ordinary. Was this her husband? The one she risked her life and her newborn child's life to come and see? Was it worth her days of misery on the freight train to find him drunk with a bunch of drunkards?

Did he care, at all, about her, or the child? Or, was it his way of dealing with pain and frustration and worry to bury his head in the sand? He was like everybody else, getting drunk and forgetting about everything.

The very next day, she took her daughter to the church to pray and give thanks for her birth, for her and her daughter's safe return, and to offer her beautiful, long, amber string to the Virgin Mary. She hanged up the long string on Virgin Mary's statue, among many gifts that people left in thanks.

Chapter 24

The Iron Curtain

1945. The war was over. The world has been divided among the great powers.

For the time being, Romania retained its Monarchy. Things were going smoothly at the Romanian schools in Salonika.

Thiana was pregnant again. She worked at the school with Costin. At home, her younger brother, Vangheli and her mother, took care of Magdalena. It was a happy and quiet time in Thiana's life. She and Costin were going out again almost every night. Her family was content, and thanks to Costin, they had plenty of everything.

When the time to give birth came, this time, Costin took her to the best hospital in Salonika and there were talks about Queen Frederica baptizing their second daughter.

It was not meant to last.

The monarch in Romania was sent away, and the communists took over. The Romanian government once again severed all relationships with Greece and closed the Romanian schools in Salonika. Costin, as a Romanian citizen, was obliged to return in Romania.

There were other possibilities open for them. They could immigrate to Australia, or even to America, but Costin was one of those rare people for whom the duty to his country came first. If the communists took over his country, he was still a Romanian and therefore that was the place he had to come back to. And of course his family, his sisters, and brothers were all there.

For Thiana, the move was extremely difficult. Her family remained in Greece. However at that time, she did not know that the separation from them was to be permanent, as all the relationships between the two countries severed for years to come.

The countries beyond the Iron Curtain were to remain isolated from the rest of the free world for better than forty years.

chapter 25

Bucharest

Costin and Thiana took a few suitcases with their clothes, their two children in their arms, and left for Romania. They traveled by train.

Again they were detained at the frontier point with Yugoslavia, in Timisoara, and questioned about their identity and reason for coming back, to Romania.

The communist regime had started to enforce their Iron Curtain policies.

It was fortunate that they remembered their colleague from Salonika, now living in Timisoara. Peia came to the checkpoint, identified them and brought them a huge bowl of chicken soup for them and the children.

Once they arrived in Bucharest, Thiana looked for a house close to the center of the city, one she would like and could live in. The apartment they owned in Maria Rosette was still rented out and occupied, not that Thiana wanted to live there.

They found and bought an old Byzantine house located near the Calea Victoriei, with thick, brick walls and high ceilings, and stucco moldings adorning each room's ceiling and doors. Wild, red roses climbed the outside walls and the black wrought iron fence.

The old proprietors of the house, two old maids, had the house furnished with antique furniture. They offered to sell the house as it was. They were anxious to move out and each to buy her own apartment. The old house had kept them together for too long.

Thiana was adamant that they should take all their old furniture out. She wanted the house empty. She wanted to buy the things and the furnishings she would like. She thought of herself, still in free Romania.

It never happened. Their school salaries were meager. The children needed clothing and food. The communist regime installed a law about properties and about how much living space each person was allowed to inhabit.

Over night, everyone had become equal. People from outside Bucharest invaded the capital and demanded living quarters. The government forced the owners to rent their houses out to people who did not have a place to live. Their old, beautiful, house was divided and each room rented to a family.

Thiana's family was forced to live in the two rooms, up front, facing the street and the main hallway leading to the rooms.

The only two bathrooms of the house were located in the back hallway near the back entrance. Now several families inhabited the house initially designed for one family.

Hard times were ahead.

Costin insisted on having one more child, in the hopes they'd have a boy to carry on the family's name for future generations.

One year later, Thiana gave birth to a son. They name him Apostol, after Thiana's brother Toli, and Radu after the Romanian Voievod, "Radu, The Beautiful."

They settled down and raised their three children. Life had its ups and downs in communist Romania. They had to suffer restrictions and hardships, like everyone else, in those years.

Thiana was constantly talking and remembering things from back in Avdela. She told her children about them.

On more than one occasion, she used to say that her only wish was to go back to her native land, Avdela, and kiss the ground.

There were many years when she could not correspond with her brothers and mother.

By 1970's the correspondence with the outside word started to be allowed and Thiana heard from her family.

She learned that her sister, Maritza, had died in a terrible accident, when her house caught in fire and she'd run inside to save her baby, and could not make it back out.

She heard about Take, who became the Mayor of Avdela and was printing a local newspaper. She heard about her youngest brother, Vangheli, who had just married.

chapter 26

Cucotul al Sioutzouki

Later in 1977, after so many denials to receive a passport, she finally got one and visited her native land. Everything had changed from what she remembered.

It had been almost thirty years since she last had been to Greece.

Her youngest brother took her for a short visit to Avdela.

Her parents' house, built on the top of the hill, was now demolished. Even the stones were taken apart and carried down into the valley, where her two brothers, Vangheli and Take, had built new houses for their wives and children.

She was now a guest in her youngest brother's house and his wife was not very friendly.

She went up to *Cucotul al Sioutzouki*, the old pecan tree, where her parents' house used to be. She sat on the only thing that remained of their old house, a big stone with minerals glinting in the sun.

She sat there, weeping over her lost youth and her lost dreams and her lost sister.

It was too late for her now. Her life was spent.

But, maybe it was not too late for her children. Maybe, her youngest daughter, Silver, would succeed where she had failed. Silver had inherited Thiana's courage and determination and her zest for life. Silver might succeed and move the family back to Greece, to Thiana's native land, Avdela, and live here.

That was Thiana's most cherished desire that her children live in a free country.

The end.

www.ingramcontent.com/pod-product-compliance
Lightning Source LLC
LaVergne TN
LVHW040157080526
838202LV00042B/3196